MATAMAI

...bring forward a vision...

You must not lose faith in humanity. Humanity is like an ocean; if a few drops of the ocean are dirty, the ocean does not become dirty.

--Mahatma Gandhi

Ang hindi marunong lumingon sa pinanggalingan ay hindi makararating sa paroroonan.

He who does not look back from where he came will never reach his destination.
--Tagalog Proverb

Ua hoʻi ka noio ʻau kai i uka, ke ʻino nei ka moana.

The seafaring body has returned to land, for a storm rages at sea.
--Hawaiian Proverb

Kaua e rangiruatia te ha o te hoe; e kore to tatou waka e u ki uta.

Do not lift the paddle out of unison or our canoe will never reach the shore.
--Maori Proverb

Pear ta ma ʻon maf. The land/ocean has eyes.

--Rotuman Proverb

MATAMAI

Intersecting Knowledge across the Diaspora

A Collection of Poems, Short Stories & Art
by Students of Pacific Islander Studies

City College of San Francisco, San Francisco State University
&
The 2nd VASA National Conference & Assembly

edited by

Kerri Ann Borja-Navarro
Richard Benigno Cantora
Andrew Fatilua Tunai Tuala
David Ga'oupu Palaita

cover art by

Vaeomatoka Valu

an ala press offering

ala

means "basket" and "nest" in the Chamorro language and "path," "fragrance," and "to rise up" in the Hawaiian language. As such, we chose to honor our press with the name Ala because of our belief that literature has the power to carry, nurture, guide, beautify, and awaken. We publish a diverse range of styles in poetry, fiction, creative nonfiction, drama, graphic novels, and children's books by writers who trace their genealogies to the native peoples of "Polynesia," "Micronesia," and "Melanesia." If you are interested in submitting a book-length manuscript, please inquire via email, pacificliterature@gmail.com.

Brandy Nālani McDougall, founder

is Kanaka Maoli (Hawai'i, Maui, O'ahu and Kaua'i lineages), Chinese and Scottish. She has worked as Editor for *'ōiwi: a native hawaiian journal* and *Mānoa* and co-founded Kahuaomānoa Press. She is also the author of a poetry collection, *The Salt-Wind, Ka Makani Pa'akai* (Kuleana 'Ōiwi Press, 2008) and a chapbook, "Return to the Kula House," featured in *Effigies: An Anthology of New Indigenous Writing* (SALT, 2009). She teaches Indigenous Studies within the American Studies Department at the University of Hawai'i at Mānoa.

Craig Santos Perez, founder

is Chamoru from Guåhan (Guam). He has worked as Editor for the past seven years for various literary journals and publishers. Additionally, he is the author of two poetry books: *from unincorporated territory [hacha]* (Tinfish Press, 2008) and *from unincorporated territory [saina] (*Omnidawn Publishing, 2010). He earned an MFA from the U of San Francisco and is currently pursuing a Ph.D. in Comparative Ethnic Studies at the University of California, Berkeley. He teaches Creative Writing in the English Department at the University of Hawai'i at Mānoa.

Contents

Acknowledgements

Borja-Navarro-Cantora-Tuala-Palaita (genealogies)

Faia'oga (teachers)

City College of San Francisco, San Francisco State University, VASA National Conference (education)

Interdisciplinary Studies, Pacific Islander Studies, Philippine Studies (knowledge)

Tangata Vasa (Village/Community)

Duwamish-Ohlone (nation)

Ala (archive)

Generations (tomorrow)

Tua'a (ancestors)

We dedicate this volume of Matamai to Rita Wesley Naputi, for helping us to remember, know, and cultivate our roots; Barbara Cantora, for showing us how to build bridges; Ofeira Fatilua Tunai Tuala, for teaching us resilience and compassion; and Alasi Ga'oupu Johnson, for sharing with us the meaning of life within love and hope. Thank you for guiding our way.

Foreword: In Retrospect

Richard Benigno Cantora
David Ga'oupu Palaita

The publication of this edition finds us at a unique place in the intersection of America and the world. The recent 10th year anniversary of the events of September 11, 2001 and the ripples that were felt throughout the world are contrasted by the "certain doom" that the year 2012 has in store not only for the United States of America, but for the entire globe. America's feeling of uniqueness on the days following horrific violence visiting its shores have had ten years to sink into our memories and understanding of what it means to exist with others ... in this world. The world wept with and for America. The U.S. paid it forward by mobilizing a response that included both global war and economic devastation. In the hindsight of the last decade how bad could 2012 really be?

Regardless of how one feels about the prognostications and predictions surrounding the year 2012, the extra seconds, thoughts and reflections we've all spent considering what lays ahead for us this year have been real. We can only imagine what the last ten years have been like for the students who have authored and produced the works in this year's edition of Matamai. Locally and globally so much has changed in the lives of students over the last ten years that perhaps this foreword would reach a broader audience as a facebook post or tweet. Of course the local and global change we reference is not limited to the lives of students, but what we wish to impress upon you is how much different being a student now is from ten, fifteen, twenty or more years ago. The new paradigm of student life requires a person to live a real, online and hybrid existence.

The works you will find here help to inform us of how students are engaging, changing, and hybridizing the events and practices that shape their lives in order to shape their ocean. For some of the authors this may be one of the few times that they have taken the time to commit to paper the thoughts and ideas which appear here. But similar to all of us, we guarantee that this is not the first time these students have taken a few extra seconds to reflect upon their lives and search for meaning that makes sense to them and their environment. Their stories are reflections of timeless realities that continue to teach us all.

When students teach in this way, we are reminded of the sacred places from which their works are drawn from. They teach us a way to see the world from multiple directions while learning to privilege their voices alongside works that are deemed authoritative. *The works here add an equally powerful and alternative view of the ever-growing complexities of our ocean in the diaspora.*

As this piece is being written, many of our communities are becoming sick, our children are dropping out of school at sky-rocketing rates, our cultures are eroding, and our languages are disappearing. But despite these massive struggles, it is our hope that this collection of student work is recognized for what it is: a needed step in moving our communities closer to the solutions we seek. The scholars of tomorrow who will help navigate the future of our communities are calibrating their compasses.

December 2011, Richmond, CA

Introduction: "Intersecting Knowledge across the Diaspora"

Kerri Ann "Ifit" Naputi Borja-Navarro
(Familian Calderon yan Familian Daso)

Being a person whose lineage can be traced back to one of the many islands of Pasefiku/a, but whose life can be traced throughout the diaspora, it is imperative that we remember, know, and cultivate our roots and find the intersections that connect us all.

Like many of our Pasefiku/a sisters and brothers living in the diaspora, we have been raised away from the island our ancestors and peoples have always called home. This was not a decision of our own choosing, nor was it entirely our parents' choice either. For most, it was the only choice they had, given the oppressive conditions and struggles happening on the island during their time. Colonization and imperialism are the root causes of the oppressive conditions and struggles that our parents faced then and our peoples continue to face currently, from Papua to Guåhan to the Marshall Islands to Tuvalu and everywhere in between. It is the work of these colonial institutions and imperialist systems found within our islands that have crippled and tricked our peoples into believing that their way is the only way, that they know best for us, and that we cannot survive without them. However, that is not so.

Our peoples are ancient and wise. We have survived on the planet for thousands of years. We navigated the largest body of water on the planet by using the ocean, the sky, and the animals within them. We shared and exchanged everything from knowledge to food to skills to arts with each other because 'ere not individualistic peoples, rather we were collective and one peoples. We were and still are, all connected to each other by the ocean and the sky. Her/his/ourstories, our language, our knowledge, our ways of knowing and learning were passed down from our ancestors since the beginning of time, through the breathe of our elders and peoples in the forms of stories, chants, and songs. It was through this, that we learned her/his/ourstory, our culture, our values, our ways of living, our native tongue, our lineage, and who we are as Pasefiku/a.

Then came the colonizers and imperialists who brought with them their knowledge, their language, their culture, their ways of learning, which were imposed and forced upon our peoples. We were lied to and denied her/his/ourstories, our culture, our values, our ways of living, our native tongue, our lineage and learning whom we truly were. Required to learn their histories, their culture, their values, their ways of living, their language, their lineage, and who we were in relation to them if we wanted to survive. They stole and occupied our islands, such as Hawai'i, Marshall Islands, and Guåhan, and turned them into a "Destination Paradise," an atomic testing site, and the largest floating military bases.

Our peoples used to learn differently before colonial institutions and imperialist systems. We sat in the ocean, on the sand, in the jungles, and on top of mountains. We shared words using our mother tongues. Our ways were hearing, seeing, feeling, and knowing. Everything we needed and learned came from the ocean, the land, the sky, and our peoples both past and present. We learned our identities as warriors, healers, dancers, chanters, storytellers, carvers, builders, navigators, womyn and men chiefs, farmers, fishers, etc. We knew our lineage of who we were, who we are, and how we are all connected. We worked together, as one, Pasefiku/a.

Now, we must pass down the knowledge and traditions, to ensure the continuity of our peoples. We must organize and take back all our stolen and occupied is/lands, for land is life. We must reclaim our language, teaching and speaking it with one another. We must preserve and perpetuate our cultures, for future generations of Chamorus, Marshallese, Maori, Kanaka Maoli, etc. We must teach our peoples the true her/his/ourstories and identities of our peoples, who are ancient and wise.

Therefore, it is essential for us to erase the lines that were created to divide our islands and peoples into Polynesia, Melanesia, and Micronesia and recover the intersections that connect us and make us one, Pasefiku/a. Then, as one, broaden our work to find the intersections that connect Pasefiku/a to all oppressed peoples and their struggles around the world. From Columbia to Egypt to Nepal to the Philippines, we must stand and fight together against colonialism and imperialism, for the true liberation and freedom of all of our peoples, both back home and in the diaspora. For what happens in one part of the world has a direct link and effect on another part, because we are all connected and bound together by the ocean.

VASĀ 2
MATAMAI

Tala/Stories: Matamai—Intersecting Knowledge across the Diaspora

In an attempt to archive the voices of students of Pacific Islander Studies in the U.S., the Matamai series—in partnership with Ala Press—was established in the spring of 2009.

This 2nd volume contains works by students enrolled in Pacific Studies courses at the City College of San Francisco & San Francisco State University during Fall 2010 to Fall 2012, and the 2nd VASA National Conference & Assembly.

"Mata" is a popular term found across all Pasefika languages denoting "eyes," "see," "vision," "watch," and "look." "Mai," another popular Pasefika term, denotes "forward," "welcome," "come," "bring," and "summon."

When the words are combined, "Matamai" is created, which translates as "bring forward a vision."

This phrase expresses/encourages one to bring visions/ thoughts/songs/poems/stories/essays/art/spoken word about the "ocean in us," the central theme of the Matamai series.

VASA

Peni Tafuna

Where do I begin, VASA...what a powerful word...I get chills
when i hear that word...VASA, meaning Sacred Space, Ocean,
space where we relate, not separate...this one word means a lot
to our people...by our people i mean the people of the
ocean...Who are the people of the ocean you may ask...we come
from all over, our population is as vast as the oceans itself...we
are the islanders spread across this earth; Polynesia, Micronesia,
Melanesia...we are stereotyped to be kept down...we aren't that
smart, we are only good for sports. or we won't be able to move
forward in real careers, only construction ('iate)...but that is
where they are wrong...and this is where VASA steps in...VASA
brings our people together so that we can see the true potential
that lies within all of us...there are endless possibilities when it
comes to the success of our people...picture a branch from the
coconut tree...there are many individual leaves on one branch, it
can't hold anything or give you shelter...but when you get all of
those individual leaves and have them woven together you
can make something like a basket to hold whatever you need to
hold or make a roof that can give you shelter...our people are
many different branches and most of the time we stand as
individuals...but VASA is what helps bring us together so that
we may be woven into something greater not as one person, but
as one people...some say that this world is moving forward, and
its moving fast...and we aren't sure if we can keep up...so what
is VASA going to do about that...my people, we can keep up
with this ever-changing world...we are capable to adapt and
move on...our ancestors were able to do it...so why can't
we...same story different chapter...VASA is going to help open
your mind...to see what you couldn't see before...if our people
can navigate through the vast oceans by jus looking up and

using the stars, then why can't we keep moving forward with this world...VASA would also remind us that we are capable to move forward and at the same time stay in touch with our roots, to remember where we came from...for when we forget where we come from, our culture slowly starts fading away and all will be lost...so keep your head up and stay strong...keep the VASA movement going, so we can rise above those who doubted...and one day we will find ourselves sitting in a circle with others from all over as equals, in peaceful unity...THIS...IS...VASA...

Indigo Waves of Emotions

Tiana Jade Palomares

A tribute to the Vasa—A poem that celebrates the Vasa and its ability to unite
and heal. We are all connected by the waves of our ocean.

Go towards the indigo waves of emotions and cleanse yourself
    of despair
The water is warm and your connection to the shore is
    magnetic.
Wrap the love of your ancestors in an embrace from your soul
And allow rays of the atomic sun to shine carelessly upon your
    face.
Hug yourself silently but realize that when you take the time to
    listen
The people are synchronizing melodies and harmonizing life.

The beauty of the Vasa is undeniable in its entire splendor
It shares the truth of the world in the sincerity of its existence
The Vasa's frequency of love is dispersed when the tide hits the
    ocean floor
It pounds with fury and comfort, and patience, and force.

When the Vasa is angry because it feels the energies of its
    people
It is noticeable in the way the waves rock the boats
She caresses you softly in a rocking motion of love
When the peace of her people is felt from below.
When the waves are invisible and the water is motionless
Her heart is calm and serene in appreciation for her daughters
And her sons who are fighting to deliver a message
To acknowledge her strength as subtle as it seems
It's her wisdom that unravels our fear, and propels our courage.

Go towards the indigo waves of emotions, and drink the water
    from the shore
Allow your internal spirit to replenish its thirst
You were thirsty to taste the raw ingredients she supplied
You were eager to gain the nutrients of the earth.
You live earnestly in abundance, as long as your soul is
    connected with the Vasa.

I am a Pacific Islander of Filipino and Asian decent, born and raised in the Bay Area, CA. My desire is to one day deliver an important message of hope through the elaboration of my words.

Ofa Ke Tapuaki'i Koe (Your Blessings)

Fahina Kolokihakaufisi

Fokutonu Lea 'e Losana Kolokihakaufisi
Translated into Tongan by Losana Kolokihakaufisi

Ha'u kiate au
Ha'u 'o tala ho'o ngaahi fiema'u
Pea fanongo ki he 'eku ngaahi tala'
Pea 'e teke fiemalie ai
He koe me'akotoa, koe tapuaki 'oe 'Otua.
Ko ia tangaki ho fofonga kiate ia
Lea 'aki 'ae lea 'oku faka'ofo'ofa'
Ha'u kiate ia 'i he iue malohi
Pea 'e hiki hake koe
Ka 'e toe mahulu ange,
Ho'o fanongo mo faka'ata
Ho 'atamai moe laumalie'

Come walk with me,
Come talk with me,
Come listen to me
And be present with me.
All you possess is a God-given blessing.

So pay attention with your wondrous eyes.
Speak up with your beautiful mouth.
Walk tall with your strong build,
And head held high.
But most importantly,
Listen with an open mind
And keep an open heart.

Otoʻota Fahina Kolokihakaufisi, also known as Fahina, is a Tongan daughter of the Pacific brought to this world by Mele Kaifonuamanu Vuni (daughter of Malina Vaka & Lisiate Filisonuʻu Vuni) of Fasi moe Ahi in Nukuʻalofa, Tonga and George Niumataʻevalu Kolokihakaufisi (son of Ana Longolongo ʻae Valu Tapealava & Samiuela Fatafehi Manupuipuiʻone Kolokihakaufisi) of Kolofoʻou in Nukuʻalofa, Tonga. Born in Philadelphia, PA, Fahina and her family moved to California in 1999 where they now live in Sacramento, CA. After graduating high school in Spring of 2010, Fahina was accepted to San Francisco State University where she stumbled upon the Pacific Islanders' Club at SFSU and their sister campus, City College of San Francisco (of whom she now calls family). Fahina was a student of Interdisciplinary Studies 45: Pacific Islander Studies Fall 2011 class, taught by Professor David Gaʻoupu Palaita and will always cherish his teachings, knowledge and wisdom. With the help of Professor Palaita and his IDST 45 class at CCSF, Fahina has realized her potential in life as a woman very proud of her Oceanic history.

Malo Eiki, malo ʻaupito moe ʻofa lahi atu.

In a Dream

Sarah Voris

In my dreams, I can see it.
The land of my ancestors, beautiful,
and so far out of reach.
But in my dreams...I can touch it.

Feel the roots of tradition under
the soles of my feet, rocky with
restriction, yet softened by mud
thick with pride and love to protect and connect...
To the soul through my feet so I'd always be
grounded by my grandparent's beliefs.

In my dreams, it's realer than anything I've
ever encountered. I am free there, at peace there
and at this rate, I hope I never wake up.

American born and raised, my roots are traced back to Upolu and Tutuila.

VASA is…

Evy Tafaifa Pati

Born into a family where VASA flows from one generation into
mine.

VASA is WISDOM.

Raised with integrity strong and true; with discipline and
religion putting God first in all that I do.

VASA is STRENGTH.

Taking back my CULTURE, TRADITIONS and LANGUAGE
that my ancestors fought to keep and so will I.

VASA is KNOWLEDGE.

Given the talent of SONG; Singing the songs that VASA carried
from my ancestors to my HEART.

VASA is MUSIC.

Put into a society where the media says that Troy Polamalu and
Dwayne "THE ROCK" Johnson are the FACE of all
SAMOAN PEOPLE.

VASA is MISUNDERSTOOD.

Trying not to be another Pacific Islander College DROP OUT
STATISTIC.

VASA is STRIVING FOR SUCCESS.

Thrown into a classroom where I'm surrounded by SAMOAN,
TONGAN,FIJIAN, HAWAIIAN, CHAMORU PEOPLE
FROM OUR SEA OF ISLANDS.

VASA is CONNECTED.

The OCEAN is the only entity that can be simple and complex
at the same time.
VASA is MULTIPLICITY.

My Name is Evelyn Tafaifa Pati Born July 31, 1989 in Ft. Benning Georgia .
I am Samoan . My Father: Livingston Pati Tauiliili from Fitiuta Manua/
Tahiti. My Mother: Tafaifa Marlene Tafao Perofeta from Ofu/Tau Manua and
Pago Pago, Fagatogo, Nuuli, Tafuna, Poloa.

Within Us

Kathleen Anne Swalve

A sea of islands,

Connected by one ocean!

Brought together through one vasa.

Fighting for one cause,

Born with in ones heart,

To revive ones culture,

For the ones of the Pacific.

With one compass,

That brings all things sacred together,

The Ocean!

I Am Me

Solouta Togiaso

Who Am I?
As I lay here wondering about what the future holds for me;
My thoughts lingered about my ancestor's future.
Who Am I?
The silent have spoken
The breeze vanished
Who Am I?
I want to know why?
What are they looking for?
Have they found it?
Can they leave us alone now?
Who Am I?
Is enough enough?
"Ia tatou ifo ma tatalo"
Are things getting better?
Oh, how I long to see your face
Who Am I?
It doesn't take long
The chains that holds me down has been broken
No more sorrow
No more sadness
No more pain
But the fire burning inside me urges to come out
Who Am I?
No more pain
No more sadness
No more sorrow
But the chains that holds me down has been broken
It doesn't take long
Who Am I?

Oh, how I long to see your face
Are things getting better?
"Ia tatou ifo ma tatalo"
Is enough enough?
Who Am I?
Can they leave us alone now?
Have they found it?
What are they looking for?
I want to know why?
Who Am I?
The breeze vanished
The silent have spoken
Who Am I?
My thoughts lingered about my ancestor's future.
As I lay here wondering about what the future holds for me;
Who Am I?
I Am Me.

Solouta Togiaso is a freshmen attending City College of San Francisco. Born from the beautiful island of Samoa, she grew up with one brother and two sisters. First came to the United States in 2001 and lived in San Diego for four years. Then in 2005, she moved with her family to Tacoma, Washington and lived there for another four years. And then in 2009 her family moved again, and now they reside in Daly City, California.

Growing Up

Lavinia Kata

What does it take to be a Tongan?
Will learning the Tongan language make you Tongan?
Learning a Tauʻolunga?
Cooking Lu Sipi, or other Tongan dishes?
Anga Fakatonga?
Fakaʻapaʻapa?

Growing up,
I've struggled with adapting
To life at home and
Life at school.
Juggling the fekaus from my parents
And school work.

Growing up,
I've grew to lose who I am,
My culture,
Due to pop culture.
But as I got older,
I have learned that
In order to get to where you want to go,
You have to know where you come from.

The Great Voyager

Samiu Alipate

My illustration of a sea turtle with traditional Polynesian designs on its shell I believe is tied to the VASA knowledge because it tells the story of all Pacific Islanders of Oceania. The illustration depicts the two front fins as flags representing the Kingdom of Tonga. Being of Tongan decent seems right to show not only that I am a member of the Tongan community but most importantly a member of Oceania/VASA. The sea turtle is known for its long trips through our ocean which connects us all. The sea turtle brings its culture and traditions to the islands it travels to. I chose to use a sea turtle because like the sea turtle, we as Pacific Islanders travelled the Ocean connecting ourselves to one another. We travel our highway of knowledge, the ocean, to spread our culture and learn of another in the vast open seas. With the traditional Polynesian designs on its shell, my sea turtle will continue to travel the world and spread awareness and knowledge of Oceania and VASA.

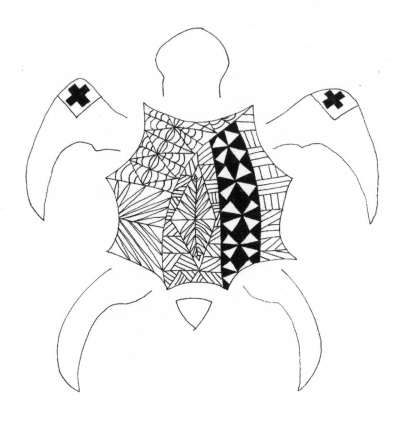

My name is Samiu Alipate and I directly identify myself as Tongan. Both my parents are originally from the Kingdom of Tonga. My mother is from Tatakamotonga and my father is from Fo'ui. My parents migrated to the U.S in the late 1970's early 1980's.

Identity

Jesse Jordan Aguilar

What am I?
How did I come this far without knowing who I am
Exactly when will I know?
Me knowing my identity does not make me who I am
No part of my being is determined by my last name.

I am a man of the ocean
I was here in America before it was known as America
I was here in 1816 and left for the islands in 1898
And once the fight was done I came back to the Americas in 1965
Settled In America

I am a product of history through the Irish in me
I am a product of culture through the Filipino in me
I am a product of pride through the Mexican in me
And although I know what I am
Exactly who am i?

I am Jesse Jordan O'keefe/Garces/Aguilar
I stand at 6 foot tall weighing in at 220 pounds
I am a man first and foremost
And although i may know what I am
Not one bit of that has shaped me into the man I am today

I am the ocean
I am calm and I crash!
I am peaceful
I am vast
I am powerful

And although I am my own entity
I connect all people
And just like tangaloa
I will raise many islands from the mighty ocean
Through my heritage
And my islands will live on through me.

My name is Jesse Jordan Aguilar. I am a Filipino/Irish/Mexican American. Growing up I never had a self-identity. My father left me at birth I was raised by my Filipino/Irish family. This piece of work should describe exactly how I feel about my identity. Thank you very much.

Unconditional Love

Lisa F. Leui

Some months ago my life didn't mean much to me,
Living life day to day without any purpose seen,
A Polynesian woman whose main focus were her children,
But she lost focus of what should've been,
As years go by lives change, people change,
Feelings of love & resentment, time to rearrange,
In our Polynesian culture family bond is sacred,
What went wrong, what could have been said?
Along came a grandson, such a wonderful blessing,
Could that have been what was missing,
The Love for this child so strong,
This family now formed a stronger bond,
Respect within our culture is always passed on,
And to this new child even after we are gone,
Our children will visit their Samoan homeland one day,
To learn more of their culture and the Island way,
Our history, our heritage, & our culture,
Will be instilled in their minds for their future,
Our culture not lost within this family,
Prayers to God for his blessings, and what is meant to be.
Dedicated to my family and my grandson, Nixon Immanuel
Tuala

My name is Lisa F. Leui and I live in San Francisco, California. My parents were both born in American Samoa, my father from Manu'a and my mother from Utulei. My dad joined the Coast Guard and was stationed in Monterey, California. From Monterey we moved to San Francisco and have been here ever since.

My Passion, My Culture, My Heart

Monique Gray

My name is Monique Gray and this is my first semester at City College of San Francisco. I was raised in Richmond, CA and have lived in the East Bay since birth. I identify myself as Filipino and Samoan. My mother is Filipino and my Father is Filipino and Caucasian. I have been blessed to be raised by my Great-Great-Grandmother, Veronica Achica Marpa, who was born and raised in Samoa.

A Way of Life

Steve Breaux

For this project I sat with writer's block for days. I couldn't decide on any poem or paper that I hadn't already written I was trying to choose something that would be a new direction to take my mind on this assignment. I finally decided that I would paint a picture. I can't remember a time I felt more proud and inspired as when I first learned about the waka trip that happened in San Francisco recently. I also learned how much our culture relied on the stars as navigation so I put the big dipper in my painting as well. I call this masterpiece <u>A Way Of Life</u>. A brief history of my mother's side. My grandfather grew up in the Philippines and joined the Navy to help serve and one of the benefits was that my grandmother, auntie Maria, my mother Lilia and him would be granted citizenship to the US. They later had another daughter Andresa and we all still live in San Francisco to this day.

In my painting there is a Vaka which to me is a key symbol of being an islander. I wanted to show how they navigate the seas so I put the big dipper in the left corner, which meant this was at night so there is a large moon helping to light the way. This experience to me shows a way of navigating through everyday experiences and helps bring me back to the basics and not get too carried away with what I think I need—a humbling experience. I want to say I am not a painter and as a matter of fact this was my first attempt but it was a spiritual experience that I am grateful for.

My Views of Bikini

Nicholas Chinn

I see Bikini Atoll island in the Pacific Ocean
Pacific Islanders forced off their homeland
A radioactive test site
Atomic bombs exploding in the Ocean
Poisoned by nuclear radiation
People suffering and dying
Belittlement of Pacific Islanders

I see our Ocean navigating us
To bring peace to our Ocean and Islands
Building of our community voices
An Ocean that is nuclear free
To remember Bikini Atoll destruction
And NOT a two-piece bikini swim suit

Nicholas is a Chinese American that was born and raised in San Francisco
CA. Nick is attending at CCSF is planning to transfer to SF State majoring in
business/computer information science. During his free time Nick likes to
explore different parts of San Francisco such as the San Francisco Presidio.

Lock Down

Betsy Otumaka

Growing up I was always told to stay home, do the chores around the house, and to always listen to my parents! I was never allowed to go out with my friends no matter how many times I begged. I always thought my dad was unfair and didn't want me to have fun! As I got a little older my dad was still strict about letting me out but in addition to my dad being over protective my boy cousins, uncles, and grandpa started to do the same! Not only was I not allowed to go out I wasn't allowed to have a boyfriend, I couldn't smoke or drink, I couldn't wear certain clothes, and I had to watch my language all the time! Compared to my friends I wasn't allowed to do anything! I was always jealous because my friends were "free" and I wasn't! When I got to high school I was still on lock down but the over protectiveness got worse! While I was at home all my friends got to go to parties and have fun and after the weekend was over I would always hear how much fun they had. By my senior year I noticed that most of the girls that I knew were either pregnant, getting messed up at parties and were doing embarrassing things, or weren't on track to graduate. I also noticed that some of those girls had brothers who didn't even care about how guys treated them or even cared about what they did! I then realized that the reason why my dad, boy cousins, uncles, and grandpa were so over protective was because they cared and because they wanted to me to hold myself with respect and didn't want me to end up like all the other girls. Although I missed out on so many parties I thank all the men in my family for caring! In the Tongan culture this is called faka'apa'apa, which means respect! I look at this as a lesson of respect for myself and for my family because if you look bad you're making your family look bad as well!

My Heart's Unbounded

Catalina Francisco

I am an American. I am Filipino. I am Spanish. I am Mexican. I am
Chamorro. Born and raised in San Francisco; yesterday, today and tomorrow.
My origins have no boundaries nor do they have borders.

Pasefika

Reo Tafa'i

A rising tide that lifts all ships to their destination

Guided by the sun, the moon and the stars without a question

Liking the neighboring islands together in unity

As one we are all aiga, ohana, familia, FAMILY

This ocean plays a big role in the lives of Polynesians

It's the resource for things of any reason

We treasure these waters that will never go away

Especially the people of Tonga, Samoa and Hawai'i Nei

Warrior

Davis Brian Maile

In the heart of the south pacific, land surrounded by the ocean
and man birthed from stone and sand, a culture of humility and
a foundation built upon the back of a savage/

Grateful to just exist, we are stimulated by simplicity and
choose a simple life of love and family over living lavish, but
yet we still wish for it/

We as a people love until no end but hate even harder so any
kindness that is taken for weakness is on a short leash because
of the beast that lingers in our veins and our souls filled with
fire so at any giving moment it can be unleashed/

That sun has rested above our islands keeping the fire inside of
us to burn continuously through generations as we have yet to
be conquered, what we lack in numbers, we make up for it in
our willingness to give it all we have, We stand together so
given scraps we share and being stepped on we continue to
stand up for we believe/

We wear ink on our bodies to symbolize our fight because from
palm trees to concrete streets we practice the art of war, the
struggle to live does not cease until we are deceased so we must
continue to push forward and live with ours scars/

Our hearts carry the weight of this cold world so we must fight until we cannot fight anymore, we can never give in or give up although change still seems so far because WE ARE WARRIORS

Ocean Haikus

Jack Luong

Powerful ocean
Humans are minorities
Have mercy on us

Respect the water
It is unpredictable
Never turn your back

Currents and tides
Flow throughout my whole body
My body is at peace

There is no way that
An object so beautiful
Can cause so much pain

My name is Jack Luong, and I am 20 years old, currently attending City College of San Francisco. I'll be a full-time student at California State University, Monterey Bay next semester. I am actually not a pacific islander but I have a lot of family (including my brother) and my best friend living in Hawaii.

Who Am I?

Tesia "Sweetheart" Tupuola

I am the coconut trees that sway back and forth with the wind.
I am the sand that sinks between your toes.
I am the ocean that cools you on a hot day.
I am the mountains that greet you.
I am the sun that peeks upon the Kaneohe Mountains and sets to
    the Waianae Valley.
I am Honolulu.
Who Am I?
I am the cold air whistling against your skin.
I am the tall buildings that stand side by side.
I am the sun that rises upon the City and sets in the valley.
I am the bridge made of gold.
I am a Raider, a Giant, and a 49er.
I am San Francisco.
Who Am I?
I walk on the sands of Waikiki to Waimea.
I walk the busy campus of City College.
I wear my tiare flower and gold bracelets freely.
I cover up in boots and jeans.
I wear my slippahs and shorts.
I talk pidgin
I speak proper English.
I am a local girl.
I am a local girl in the city.
I am Samoan, Tongan.
I am Polynesian.
I am Tesia "Sweetheart" Tupuola.

Tesia "Sweetheart" Tupuola is the daughter of Sefo Tupuola Jr. and Iulieta Lauti-tupuola, from the villages of Fagasa , Am. Samoa and Vatia , Am. Samoa. Sweetheart was born and raised in Honolulu, HI , moved to San Francisco and attends City College of San Francisco in hopes of graduating with an Associate's degree and pursuing her career in ethnic Studies. This short poem symbolizes her as an ordinary island girl and carrying pride of who she is, no matter where she goes.

Sea-ing with our Hearts

Kayla Montiel

See the sky above and the ocean below
Places, Faces, traditions, are just the beginning of what we
know
Space and time sharing the same purpose
For confining our knowledge to one era or location is worthless
How can we sustain our experiences
And let the outsiders be aware of it?
For so long our thoughts haven't fully been our own,
Swimming through and sifting through
colonization, trying to find our heritage alone.
If seeing is believing, then they must be blind
For all our stories have been passed down,
our blood and ties are what binds.
colonization, the epitome of confine Meant
to strip us of ourselves
and all we may represent
but the fact that we're still standing here
is a testament to our relevance See
the family, food and Fale
we gather in love and song
Truth as evidence of experience
doing life together in sacred space.

See the sky above and the ocean's depth
let us prevent cultural deterioration until nothing is left
Let us revitalize our unity as a sea
so outsiders will See the beauty of Poly
But more so for us, for our reunion of identity
Identity in the roots and the Sea entity.
Look beyond the limits of books

Engage all our senses to envelope our past, present and future relatives
emulate the movement and presence of the Ocean
the presence is not stationary, but in continuous motion
Borderless in space, so too, will we be borderless in love
to emulate the blessings received from above
Sea-ing is believing, as we have been doing for so long
Multi-centered, Multifaceted, collectively in song
And dance and story and action and speech
drawing from the power found in humanity
Replenishing and adding to the archive of knowledge in Oceania
taking back and preserving the presence of Pasefika

Monologue of a Queer Pacific Islander

Sifa Ataveifoa-Riley Latu

Often times when dad wasn't looking, I used to corner my
attraction for boys and
vigorously shake them...

Ofa mai, I would implode!

Kataki mai I would ask. but still no avail

So, the daily deprivations kept on coming

Whack!

take it back

Smack!

give it back! and so on, and so on

It wasn't until that day he said: Ofa atu that I cracked...

So Ofa mai, I cried and cried

Sifa Ataveifoa-Riley Latu is 1st generation Tongan-American and has been living in San Francisco since 2008. Growing up queer and Pacific Islander in Minnesota, Latu learned at a young age the importance of voice. Currently pursuing his Bachelors degree and working full time, he is an avid progressive thinker and a strong leader within the Pacific Islander and Queer Diaspora.

Pacific Islander Studies

Ryan Mosely

If there is anything that is most important to Pacific Island culture, is that family is above anything else. The bond that we have with the people around us as we grow up is what keeps us as human beings in our society. Any problem that a family member succumbs to in our lives is felt through each and every family member. In unity (as the rest of the culture thrives off of via Vasa) the family endures the pain life through each other, with also the joys in life that we share with each other. In the Vasa community in my culture, everyone is considered family and even in conflict, we find ways to find balance with each other.

My family in my life has endured a pain that unified us in one situation that no one would wish upon anyone, cancer. My mother was diagnosed with breast cancer in 2004, in which brought fear of what would lay in the future for her, along with the rest of my family. At that point in time, from an outside perspective of those who aren't considered your family, there are apologize from friends and co-workers that have thoughts of nothing but sympathy. But from my family's perspective, there are feelings of sympathy, fear, and hope; along with thoughts of what direction of our lives are going to be going into from this overwhelming experience. This is a situation that happens no matter what, and changes us as people completely within an instant. A person only has one mother that has given birth to them, no one else. It's a bond that no one else (except your siblings) can share with you in your life to the closest extent.

In time, my mother went through chemo therapy treatment. She was very ill afterward and I, my brother, and my father took care of her. Luckily for my mom, we found out that she only suffered from stage one of the cancer, which was depleted from her breast after the chemo therapy. This was a feeling of relief that I have never felt in my life and ever will hopefully. From this point on, my mother started taking care of herself via diet and exercise. This whole situation brought my family together more than anything else that has ever happened and for that I am thankful for my culture's values of unity.

My name is Ryan Mosely, age 22, cultural family roots come from the Philippines, and I live in San Francisco, California. I grew up in Pleasanton, which is east bay of San Francisco, where my father (Roderick Mosely), mother (Jocelyn Mosely), and my younger brother (Joseph Mosely) live.

Ako, Me, I

Virginia Mancenido

I am me,
No one can tell me to be otherwise,
They come into my land and say that I do not know anything,
But I do,
I know that they are trying to change me,
Trying to make me see in a different way,
They say that their way is better,
It will make you a better person,
But making me a better person makes me change,
When I start to change I forget who I am,
Forget where I came from,
Forget where my homeland is,
Then I start dressing and talking like them,
Start wanting the same things,
Coming back to the land I came from it makes me realize what I
    changed into,
What I left behind,
The family and tradition,
The things that they have taught me when I was younger,
To live off the land,
But then that land is gone and buildings come up,
Hotels are now lining what used to be free land and ocean,
Now my land has changed,
Now they forgot what it used to be like,
The traditions,
The love we had for the land,
Now we have to change,
To survive in this new land,
The land I used to call home is now changed,

Will continue changing,
But we will continue keeping our love for the land we have lost.

I am a Filipina that grew up here in the United States; both of my parents are Philippines born and speak fluent English, also graduated with Masters Degree. I grew up in Sacramento Ca, where Pacific Islanders were not common back in the 1990s.

Our Ocean

Jerelle Aquino

Water, water, can I have a little bit of water
because todays a day where the weather's a little hotter
Just a little cup, just a little sip
even just a drop 'cause I wouldn't mind it
When Im thirsty, I really shouldn't play
'Cause I needa stay hydrated every single day
Humans need to drink, so do animals, we all know-
in order to survive we need H2O
Take a look at the Earth, it's mostly filled up with ocean
Water moves freely, it's smooth with its motion
The ocean that I'm from, is the Pacific
And many different island share the Ocean to be specific
Each island has differences but all completely relate
All share culture, knowledge, and beauty that await
Another thing about the Pacific Islands for sure
That just like water, it's a place so pure

My Ocean, your ocean, flowin' real smooth it's our ocean
My Ocean, your ocean, treat it real good it's our ocean

Jerelle Aquino was born in Manila, Philippines on January 19, 1989. He is
mixed with about three quarters Filipino. He moved to San Francisco when
he was a one year old boy and was raised in San Francisco. His girlfriend is a
beautiful Tongan woman.

My title, My name

Asi Losa Afuhaamango

Sitting in my room, reminiscing on the old days.
Remembering back on how I used to be made fun of, because
     my name was different.
My name wasn't "English", my name didn't sound right.
Like soil on the ground my name stuck to me.
People always called me the little "Samoan" girl.
But I am not Samoan, don't get it twisted, but yes I am
     Polynesian
But my people have an island of their own.
I am Tongan, I love my Tongan heritage.
Although it always didn't start off that way.
I grew up and people always asked me what I was,
Because my skin was brown and my name sounded funny.
They always asked "Are you Samoan?" because of my name.
But without asking me they labeled me, and for years I went on
     with being known
As the "Samoan" girl and I began to accept the title
Even though I was not of any Samoan decent.
As years changed, I began to grow.
I went to my family reunion, and this year was different.
My father and his brothers and sisters were hosting the event.
My aunts wanted me and all my other girl cousins to learn to
     tau'alunga
A Tongan dance.
For months we practiced our dances.
My aunt was hard on us and wouldn't let us eat or rest,
Until the she said the tau'alunga was good.
When the day came I seen many people.
Many faces I recognized and many faces I did not.
But with love for a name we all came together.

Under a name we became united and were one as a family.
Under one name we shared it, and no one was ashamed of this
name.
They held the name Afuha'amango and were proud of it.
Not only were they proud of the name
But of their skin color.
They were proud to be Tongan.
They held their pride in their heart and wore it like a sleeve.
Like hear on my head my name is a crown.
Like clothing on my skin I wear my name.
Like good music to the soul I listen to my name.
I wait to hear it and when it's called it gives me strength.
My name gives me another day to be known by people.
My name is Tongan.
Tongan is my blood.
It's the language that rolls off my tongue.
It's the food that is blocking arteries.
It's the culture that moves within me.
It's the me that was always waiting to be shown.
I was Tongan since day one and have been Tongan all my life.
I am living my life as a Tongan, and I will die Tongan.
Nobody can take that away from me.

My name is Asi Losa Afuhaamango born and raised in San Francisco, California. Both my mother and father are from Tonga but from different islands. My mother is from Ha'apai and my father is from Vava'u. My father came to America when he was a teenager whereas my mother came here later during her early twenties. My mother and father knew each other because they attended the same school. They met up again in America and got married here. I am the youngest out of my family, having two older brothers. I attended San Francisco high school and graduated 2010 and am now attending City College of San Francisco.

Dreams and My Prize

Shoaib Ahmad

They can't take my dreams away!
Many of us dream, dreaming is the one thing I know for sure
     they can't take that away.
Some of us come into to the world thinking that our way of life
     is the way to live.
Our culture's traditions bring us together during time in need.
When someone comes into our land and tells us that we are
     indigenous, our way of life isn't Christ like.
Things like that cause stereotypes among our community to
     expand within ourselves.
Things in life become according to the "White" eye. The world
     is seen, yet has lost in its own way.
Yet we strive to become more like the white eye.
But I often wonder with this day in time with our technology
     become our worst enemy?
I miss the dancing & singing
But one thing is to remember they can't take your dreams away!
Still I rise. They can't take my dream away! I am gunna keep
     my eyes on the Prize!

My name is Shoaib Ahmad. But everyone knows me as Prince. I am from
Virginia. I recently moved to California from the east coast one year ago. I
came to California to pursue my dream of Hollywood. When I moved here I
thought I would be able to make it in the modeling and acting industry easily.
However, it's been a challenge considering I am not "perfect image" they
want me to be. Being a part of Pacific Islanders studies has made me
appreciate my background more. I am bi-racial; my mom is from Pakistan
and my dad is from Mexico. When audition for stuff I won't be told of by my
color, sexuality, background and overall poor judgment over looks and etc.. I
am currently at City College, looking forward to transferring to SFSU or
UCLA and pursuing Psychology and Film. I would like to move to LA and
eventually start my own line of clothes and get into reality TV. But more so
break any stereotypical barriers for everyone!

Waves of Thought

Carmina Wijayapala

With a mind of it's own
it's still,
silent,
calm.
It's relaxed and shows beauty.
As soon as you throw some sand
that pebble,
this rock,
it makes vibrations yet you cannot tell
good or bad.
Just vibrations that move along into the far distance.
All the way to the left,
to the right,
everywhere.
A little boy tries to use his hand to stop the waves.
Does this work?
No.
It has no boundaries,
the vibrating waves keep going.
It doesn't stop for no one.
It makes no judgments.
There are no bad people, no good people, no brown or white
peoples.
It only knows you as people,
period.
It affects you in the west
east
south
north.
It connects you,

us,

from all over.

We are impacted.

We live off it, we need it, we have it.

Do we appreciate it? Do we understand it?

How it does the greatest job of all.

The job to connect what we people cannot see, but what some can feel.

There is a storm.

Now you don't glisten, now you aren't at peace.

There's something that has stopped you're path.

Something that has caused you to belittle yourself.

Do you wait on the shore for the storm to pass?

You need to get to that food for your family,

you need to get on your boat.

You need to overcome the storm

You need to support your family.

Do you wait on the shore for the storm to pass?

You need to finish school,

you need to get that degree,

you need to overcome the storm

you need to support your family.

The largest archive

take your pick.

Find your own stories, next to someone else's.

Stories of the past, that frame our present.

Respect the book.

Respect the stories embedded.

Share.

How can one person take care of something so big?

So VAst?

VA.

Space.
Relation without Separation.
No Isolation
within our world's
Rotation.

My knowledge is power.
My power is in me
& I am within
I am apart of
I live off of
I respect.
the power of

our ocean.

My full name is Carmina Dela Cerna Wijayapala. I'm am American born, but
my family is from the Philippines. I was born and raised in San Francisco
under a family full of Filipino traditions. I love the Filipino culture. I used to
go back to my mother's homeland every year.

I Am the Ocean

Roxie Cherie Fuller

I am the Ocean and the Sea,
The moon shines and sparkles on top of me,
I am home to many tropical fish and many different sea
     creatures,
You will never be able to count all of my beautiful features,
From my waves to my splashes I make lots of things wet,
With me you will never have to fly in a plane or a jet,
I am home to many islands in the Pacific but my favorites are
     Tonga and Fiji,
There they have a gorgeous waterfall and an exotic flower,
But no matter what I still have all the power,
I can cause tidal waves and do some major damage,
So don't ever cross me the wrong way,
I am the ocean and the Sea,
And I will say this, if you piss me off Don't Cross Me.

My name is Roxie Cherie Fuller and I'm 22 years old. I was born in San Francisco, CA to Roscoe Fuller from Texas and Tanice Harris from Georgia.

The Islander in Me

Heilala Sema

I was born in America from a Tongan mother and Samoan father. I grew up
what most people can call "Americanized" but I knew the meaning of my
culture and identity from my family making me a proud Pacific Islander.

Misplaced Hate

Alyssa Wishman

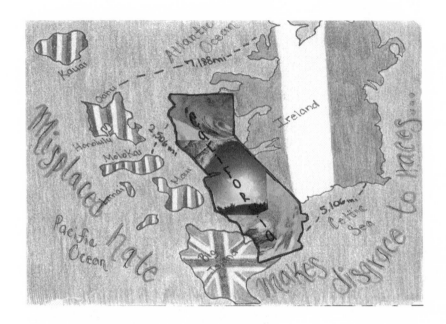

My Name is Alyssa Wishman. I am 18 years old and I was born in
California. My family comes from Ireland and Hawai'i. I have never been in
touch with my culture from either side and I hope to change that. I know very
little about both countries and cultures because my family doesn't practice
anything, not even religion. My goal is to learn about where I come from so I
can pass it on to my family.

Ocean in Us

Martin del Rosario

Life started in the Ocean....
The Ocean separates us....
The Ocean is between us....
The Ocean is in each and every one of us....
The Ocean is within us....

We are one, we are the same....
,but different....
that's what makes us all unique....
Everything can change in a second so don't blink....
Some things in this world just makes me think....
about....
the Past, the Present and the Future....
the Past is happening in the Present, they say that learn from the
Past, but what if the Past is the Future....

Yeah, I am the Ocean, The Ocean and I are one....
My Blood is like Water flowing through my veins....
,but my Mind is blank and so far gone....
Tidal Waves is my frustration and pain....
Sweating bullets because of the heat of the Sun....
Even if I'm long gone....
I will never be forgotten....
because memory is the gift that will never rotten....
if you think that this is just the beginning....
Let me remind you that....
I am the Ocean....
The Ocean is flowing through me and this is never ending....

My name is Martin del Rosario, 20 years of age, born and raised in the Philippines. Fluent in Tagalog and a full blooded Filipino whose parents came from two different regions of the country with different dialects: Bisaya and Ilocano. Migrated to U.S back in 2004 when I was 14.

Go to School

Andrew Vai

...i was in a college classroom and the professor asked the class
"raise your hand, if you would kill for your family?"
like wild west quick draw, it took me no thought
i raised my hand high stretched like the tower of babylon
        reaching for the heavens
but was i the only one to raise my hand in this class?
naw, all hands in the class was raised like we was hailing a
        dictator
he replied "im assuming its all out of love, huh?"
we all nodded our heads proud to hold it down for our families
ready to attack, wishing somebody would bring harm to our
        folks
but back lash would come so fast as the professor replied
"then why cant we learn for our families? huh? why cant we we
go to school for our families?
what does skipping school do for your family? does that help?
how about killing? tell me what does it do?"
and the only thing that was on my mind was my peoples
high school statistics in the city say pacific islanders are one of
the smallest populations in the school district
but yet are among the highest in dropout rates
and i cant understand this because i see potential in my people
like seeing the sun when it sets, you cant ignore it
i cant ignore the saturday afternoon games young uso's play to
get that scholarship for college
i cant ignore the melody of three part harmony sang over live
        acoustics by my young pi sisters
i cant ignore pi artist hidden in history class creating
        masterpieces
on pieces of papers that they should be taken they notes on
i cant ignore the slice of humble pie my brothers and sisters

share with each other
i cant ignore how the cops ignore our potential and instead
          racial profile
i cant ignore being ignored by society
because society has already set our standards and these
standards are lower than hell
knowing that we were brought in to this world with standards
          unlimited
were encouraged to do okay but thats not okay because we were
destined to be something great
seeing a future as a soldier more likely then a future in the
classroom doesnt cut it for me
so wake up pi people because we making moves out here
city college of san francisco is making moves out here
i say it loud and clear what are you going to do out here
we got this long road of life dont spend it living in fear
we navigated through the south pacific using the stars and the
          motherland as our compass
gifted speakers know to move mountains the history of leading
          is in our blood
im a pacific islander physically intimidating with a hidden heart
          of gold
moved by love never by intimidation
originators of the tattoo, pioneers in sea exploration, i am a
wordsmith continuing the oral tradition
of our ancestors telling you to wake the fuck up, acknowledge
          your potential
and be what you want to be, be a teacher, a preacher, a lawyer, a
          chef
an artist, a doctor, a poet, your best
and next time the professor ask "raise your hand, if you would
kill for your family?"
the answer next time will be "why would you even ask me that
question because right now im too busy
living it up for my family…

The Best of Both Worlds

Glareme M. Togia

The best of both worlds
The better of the two
Samoan and Black
To myself I will always be true

The best of both worlds
The best of the races
The strongest of people
The relation of spaces

The best of both worlds
Both rhythm and grace
The movement of my body
The expression of my face

The best of both worlds
The beauty of dark and light
The loveliest of mixtures
And a wonderful sight

The best of both worlds
My culture is key
One goes back thousands of years
The other taken from me

The best of both worlds
Both genuine and true
The heart of a lion
Such a beautiful virtue

The best of both worlds
Connected to the land and the sea
Both Samoan and Black
A race I am proud to be

The best of both worlds

I am of mixed decent, Samoan and black. My father is from American
Samoa, the island of Ta'u Manu'a, and the village of Fitiuta. He came to San
Francisco in the year 1971. My mother is African American, and she is from
Atlanta, Georgia.

They Had a False Run

Phaktra Long

The future for us Guahans are slowly coming to an end. These last couple of months have not been the easiest. We have encountered more bad news than good news. We have been faced with many restraints by the United States that have caused us to put a damper in our country. The United States have signed a treaty that has barricaded us from being free people. Because of the restriction, we are not able to practice our culture which we hold dear to our hearts. Our culture is what past generations teach to future generations. By not allowing us to follow our traditions, we will slowly forget about the true meaning of being a Guahan. Soon the cultures of Guahans will have been forgotten and the future generations' will not know who their ancestors were. By taking our freedom away, not only is the United States taking away our freedom, but they are slowing wiping away what is left of the Guahan.

"Forever and ever never ever is forever and ever"

Nothing good lasts because death makes sure of it.

It Has No Title

Guahan, Guahan,
Guahan, help me,
Chamoru, Chamoru,
Help me please,
Help me please,
To just believe,
That when the territories of the United States said,
"They won't establish civilian government"
Was something real,
Real as on December 8, 1941, when Japan bombed the
Island,
Same day as Pearl Harbor,
Not something crazy
Broke Guahan's heart.
Not to play them, not to shove them.
But after all the lies and tears,
I now know what I truly fear.
It is not death, not pain, nor life.
But I fear to find a real paradise.
For what is reality, when I thought it was them?
They who crushed Guahan,
United States surrendered in two days.
Chamoru insular guards fights the Japanese on
"Liberation Day"
Took away my reality?
One who promised that they'd never leave
One who promised, in Guahan, they'd
Always believe.
One who promised to be a forever and ever
I look at the grey skies now knowing it'll be forever never,
Everything was just a lie, a fake, a scam.
I'm here, lost, confused, and still don't understand.

Guahan questioned them, they lied to Guahan,
Was less than dirt
United States told them things that did not go hand in hand.
And the biggest of them all,
US Military occupies and control one third of the
Island,
With the most air able farmland and most beautiful
Beaches
Promised them in such a way that'll drive Guahan mad
Said they will not make this forever and that you'd
Never make Guahan sad.
Why did they say all those things?
When all they did was turn their backs and had a
US Naval Base.
I'm sick and tired of praying, Guahan.
I'm sick and tired of seeing, what they have done.
I know your past, I know it well.
It still haunts me, on it, I dwell.
Knock down to the status consequences of Political,
But the US culture influence, not a punishment that fits their
death?
With a slow death of the Chamoru language and culture,
That Guahan died not by their right hand, but their left
I'm broken and shattered in such a tattered mess,
Down because to the homelessness, privatization, and the
pollution.
Guahan death I admitted, to them, I swear.
No longer can I wed US to be the solid that can
My hero.
So Guahan, Guahan, Guahan help me now,
Chamoru, Chamoru,
Help me please, To just believe
That out of all things US said and has done,
That they love Guahan for real and that their love
Was well lived.

That out of all the times the Military Occupation and
Build up impact and
Current Military expansion and build up.
That they loved Guahan really and that was not a lie.
That ever invasion of the island, was not purely and truly.
Not to play and shove Guahan and manipulate cruelty,
That every thing was sweet and sincere.
I see how now it became,
and see that I was just speaking into a mirror
The US kept their memories and
Was holding it in a sorrowful of regrets,
They now realize how it impacts all the islands
I feel that my heart's tears have cleared
And that in a thousand years.
When we've all died and our bodies have withered away,
In heaven,
We'd find our way and apologize of our wrong doing.

A Voice from Guahan...

Donel Finks

They shed the blood of our people on our soil; they destroy our resources just to build a military base for their men to call home. They move us around like pawns on our island and they tell us we're not allowed to be in certain places but this is our land. They tell us we can't speak our native language but we have to learn theirs because it's the correct way. People don't have a voice here; we're like mice. The people want their land back and want the intruders to leave. Our people just want our land back; we just want to restore our land.

My name is Donel Finks. I am currently at CCSF. I am a first year student. I am African American. I love to play sports and hang out with friends. I really like the Pacific Island Studies class and I would like to learn more about the Pacific cultures.

Fa'e

Isaiah Teputepu

E Otua ke tapuaki si'eku fa'e,

Kene ma'u ha nonga mo ha fie'malie.

Si'o le'o na'a oku kei ongo mai pe,

Ho lakanga oku ma'uhinga taha pe

Heavenly father bless my mother,

So that she may have no worries and be happy,

Listen to my voice that only you can hear,

What you've done for me is the most important thing in life.

This is very much relevant to the Vasa (ocean) because we want our Heavenly Father to continue blessing our mother lands and where our roots first began. We want our mother to be a land with no worries and to kick back and stay happy. In our land, it only turns to our father for guidance and help, so what we have and continue to get, we will be satisfied. Thank you Heavenly Father for all you have given and what you will give us.

Moana

Alika Kamaile

The ocean is a never ceasing body, it carries with its tide, the circulating abundance
of life the world has to offer whether in the water, or on land, or in ourselves. The lines between the three are different from each other but we share similar obstacles. They are all struggling to survive and live in peace. The ocean in us and its entirety is a beautiful place to live if we nurture it and make it beautiful. With allowing the wars and differences (no matter the kind), rule our life no one can be complacent or even happy. Through compromise and ease we are able to get through the roughest time in this moving body. We are one but we are the same. We've got to carry each other through all our struggles and disagreements. Peace, in keeping the never ceasing body of the ocean in us, alive.

My name is Alika Kamaile I was born and raised on the Island of Oahu of the Hawaiian Island chain. I moved to the Bay Area twelve years ago. I've traveled the world while being a flight attendant for nine years, while residing in the bay. I am now enrolled in the Pacific Islander Studies course, instructed by Professor David Palaita. Aside from my studies, I am employed here in the bay area to earn a living.

He Oku Lelei

Peata "Mona" Otumaka

Eiki teu i fe, kapau e ikai teke kau mo au
He ko ho aofinima na'ane pukepuke au
Neu he he tele'a oe mate Eiki e
ka kuoke ha'u o faka'haofi au

He oku lelei ae Afiona pea oku ta'engata
Ene folofola pea mo ene alo ofa
ki he to'u tangata moe to'u tangata
he oku lelei ae Afiona pea ta'engata

Eiki e lelei kia au a ho'o ngaahi fekau
Ne faka'ofofau ae me'a na'ake fai ma'aku
Neu alu lototo'a o ikai teu tuenoa
Ka kuou ilo'i ko koe ae vai faka'nonga.

An Ocean in all of Us

Zohaib Khan

On earth everything has a rhythm, one most notable is the ocean to humans and living creatures. The ocean has always been in us, from calm ripples to the tsunamis. The majority of any living being is water as well the majority of the earth is water; however, we do not just have water but also its many attributes. What causes waves is outside pressure; winds. Our thoughts in analogy motivate our being and state. Calm thoughts cause people to be calm and relaxed like gentle waves while thrill seekers prefer turbulent inertia of strong waves. Then comes the Tsunami, a spectacle not caused by it, but by seismic quakes from under the sea and when cut loose at the shore causes great destruction.

Calm waves reflect our calm thoughts when one wants to relax. These waves are caused by the slow wind speed at sea. When we are calm it is easy to sit back and relax, the calm energies in our head make it easy for us to do just that. At night the ocean waves are calm just like us after a busy day, and it becomes easy to relax for the upcoming day ahead. This part of the ocean will always be there as long as there is day and night, age may play a factor in our well being but the need for rest will always be there.

The ocean has many types of waves making us apart of it, waves containing high energy are more turbulent due to higher wind speeds. These waves are perfect for surfing, using the oceans to satisfy our desire to seek thrill while containing the energy we want to exert. The waves, just like ourselves cannot stay in this high energy state throughout much of the day and the waves like us must come to a resting state like the people who want to ride them. The waves will always be there just as those thrill seeking energies are in us and even though they will always be there we may not, at some point in time, but the experience will remain in with us.

Tsunamis are similar to belligerent actions because such a great amount of force is used, and the target is indiscriminate of anything. Waves as tall as buildings come not from wind but the earth beneath. Leaders have waged wars from the dawn of time and like Tsunamis, they are not frequent. Bill Fernandez, a native of Kapaʻa Hawaiʻi also a judge who was appointed judge by Governor Reagan in 1969, states in his book <u>Rainbows over Kapaʻa</u>, "None of these men envisioned the consequences of defeat nor did the victors appreciate the aftermath of global war." The outcome of wars is grim as the outcome of tsunamis.

Waves of the ocean describe us humans and animals perfectly. The waves describe the ocean in us through the energies it exerts. Waves are only a small part of the ocean; much more can be explained about us being a part of the ocean and the ocean in us. The unknown depths of the ocean meet our human nature of curiosity and exploration of the unseen aspects of life. The life in the ocean describes our will to keep nature and rain forest living and to keep animal habitats intact. Humans can be described as oceans and the ocean as humans. That so few other known phenomenon can better describe us, makes the ocean a part of us.

I am not, yet I feel, and I wish

Elizabeth Zlochevskaya

Though I am not of the Pacific Islander Decent.
Though I do not come from the same struggles.
Though I see the world from different angles.
I still feel.
I feel the pain behind the voices that speak of injustice.
I feel the sadness of those who lost their home.
I feel the emptiness that comes from those who are
discriminated against.
I feel the anger that arises from the stereotypes.
And its saddens me so deeply.
Though I am not of the Pacific Islander decent.
I still see.
I see the devastation of entire islands.
I see the hope fleeting from people's eyes as military takes
charge.
I see the struggles and the progress.
I see battles won, and I see battles lost.
I see the real beauty of the Vasa and all the knowledge it has to
offer.
I see ways, other than my own, of learning, documenting, and
preserving culture.
And I wish.
I wish everyone else could see what I see.
I wish everyone else would feel what I feel.
I wish everyone else would try to learn, accept and understand
the way I have tried to.
Though not everyone is of the Pacific Islander decent.
I do not feel nor see why they can't embrace the beauty of the
different cultures.
Yet I still wish

That one day, the world will open their eyes the way mine have been opened.

My name is Elizabeth and I was born in Odessa, Ukraine and migrated to the U.S when I was 5. I am not Pacific Islander, but I am interested in the culture, which encouraged me to take Professor David Ga'oupu Palaita's course on Pacific Islanders in the United States. This course has opened up my eyes greatly on the issues that the Pacific Islander community faces, and was the inspiration for my poem.

The Challenge of Being _____-American

Kristina Salazar

America; land of the brave, home of the
    Freedom to be all that we can be
America; the beautiful
    It boasts; proud
    Harmonious of people with mountains and
    Field(s) of
    The American Dream(s)
But my America didn't boast of sunshine or people with gold
hair.
The sky had fallen in my America, but snow did not; the sun
shone, but it rained more
I traded Manila Bay for San Francisco Bay
    45 Pesos for 1 Dollar
    Pilipino for Filipino
    Sampagita for Irises
    Roots for Identity
    …
Sacrifices come and go with turn of seasons
Struggle to change yourself, while maintaining yourself;
contradictory; battle of butting heads
To be all that you can be, but don't forget to fit within; Who are
you, really?

Freedom? Haiku

America freed
My face remained although
Tides, they washed away

Good Morning Haiku

Mabuhay tayo!
Kaibigan, sumayaw!
But don't forget 'me'

Good Night Haiku

Good night, little one
Tomorrow is one more day
Seize it; life is yours

Kristina Salazar was born by the bay in the Manila, in Luzon – the biggest island of Philippines. At seven years old, she found herself in a plane with mother and two younger sisters bound for SFO to, "seize the American opportunities," reuniting with their father for new life in America.

Tanka for the Ocean

Nikol Juarez

Blue, color of my soul
Vast with knowledge, is my mind
Deep, heart filled with love
Just like the ocean, so true
Ocean is in me and you

Nikol Juarez was born on March 22, 1990. She is Mexican American and was born and raised in Santa Ana, California. She now lives in San Francisco, California and is attending City College of San Francisco. Her major is Communicative Disorders. She is hoping to transfer to San Francisco State University in the fall of 2010.

As I Grow

Mika'le Aalona Majit

As I grow, I find more about myself and my culture
I find how it continues and never ends like our seas
Even at the end of the line, I will find a new path and reconnect
to what belongs to us, our family's, our ancestors and to our
mother earth.

As I grow, my strength becomes more mental than physical. I
soon adapt to the stereotypes and the oppressed society that
holds me down and keeps me away from our freedom, from our
dreams and goals.

As I grow, I see how everything works and what doesn't, it hurts
me though that how I sit down and thinks about what is wrong
and right, but yet I am not strong enough to get up and make a
change. Why? That is something I cannot answer

As I grow, I identify myself as Polynesian, Hawaiian, to be
exact. But yet I'm still adding to the title that was giving to me
and my people. It hurts to see we are all in a group and not
considered people. Human; I apologize for being all over the
place, all my ideas and thoughts. But it's that what makes me
and our people strong, we have the mind set on what we want,
and what we deserve not only as people, but as a community in
the world.

As I grow, I soon find out that I have not grown enough.

Our vasa for knowledge are as infinite as space, it's time for us
to explore. And what we find and consume is up to us.

I apologize for being all over the place. But there is no such thing as a confinement.

My family is from Oahu, Hawai'i. We are Hawaiian blooded, but I am from all over the Bay Area, California. I was raised with my grandpa and my grandma in Milpitas, CA. There I was exposed to the food, music, love, and family from all over the islands and other cultural backgrounds. My grandpa was a real example of a family man, an islander. Now I am real close to Polynesians and most of my friends are Samoan and Tongan. I love my peoples and those who love me. They have always welcomed and love me. Thank you to all.

Ke Mla Obes (Forgotten's Lost)

Chasmon Ongeu Tarimel

Ke mla obes?
Did you forget?
When we use to be one?
A giant nation, a population, in different locations
Helping & guiding each other
In a time where the ocean was not there, nor neither
A time where our lands connected as one
Breathing the same wind & air, lost into oblivion

Like the lost continent that connected the Natives of the
    Caribbean
A land they say is myth and "so-called" existed in time,
A land called Atlantis
You probably don't know this
But We Pacific peoples also had a continent before this
Before the ocean rose, the fishes swam, before we navigated on
    canoes

In our stories, we called it Mu, Lemu'ia, Emungs, or what is
    known now as Lemuria
A land lost in time, only maintained through legend
Where we truly were united Oceanian people connected

But now, we are not
We have truly forgotten who we are
Temporarily gone, the chain that held us together
The forgotten knowledge that proved we were brother and sister

In the words of Pohnpeian poet Emelihter Kihleng
"MICRONESIA, POLYNESIA, MELANESIA

colonial constructions
colonial creations
imaginations
configurations
divisions of our Pacific Islands"

Can we now understand what this has done to our nation?

Not the nation of America, but the nation of Oceania
A nation of intelligent brown men and women
Whom are not inferior nor less than the colonial conundrum
Finding a place in this American space
Separating who is whom from what islands are not
Begging to be accepted from people who forgot
Forgotten who they are, the roots planted so deep
Makes you want to cry a little, weep weep weep

Does anyone here know the islands of Melanesia?
Never spoken of, like people got amnesia
A racist term to describe and tell those people "You are
    Black!"
Never thought of as PIs because of the color of their back.
The islands consist of Vanuatu, New Caledonia, Solomon
    Islands, Fiji
& Papua New Guinea, never to be ceased but remembered in
    eternity
Welcome them with open arms because they are family

Micro-nesia, an identity that I hate, matter of fact literally
    resent it
I am not Micro, miniscule, ignored, overseen, neither lazy nor
    stupid
An identity forgotten, spit on, discriminated against for our
    colorful skirts and red lips

Do I look Micro to you? At six foot two? I don't think so foo!
I'm Belauan, a rich island culture rarely heard
But if you had privilege to know Where I'm From through my
    eyes
You'd be lost in its tranquil paradise
Eating ngikel, ongraol everyday
Chanting to our ancestors, thanking them for the path Ng huei

And to all my "Polynesian" brothers and sisters
Who are here today, prideful in their "Poly" culture
The majority, well "respected", "represented" of this American
    nation
Please, I humbly ask you
Do not neglect your brothers and sisters on the opposite
    spectrum
Because the next time you say "Polys" to our Vasa islanders
Know that I can't be there 'cuz I'm not in that triangle
Yea, you say it's just words and it's not your intention
But sometimes, it's a form of PI discrimination

I hope you have listened to what I've said
'Cuz these colonial terms need to be dead
We were once in unity and we still can be
'Cuz I got love for my Oceania family
We live in a blind society.
So open up your eyes to the ugly that resides,
in the heart of the demise,
where you see your people RISE,
bringing justice to the colonized!

One day, One day, One day

Matisyahu
"Sometimes I lay under the moon
And thank God I'm breathin'

Then I pray don't take me soon
'Cause I am here for a reason
Sometimes in my tears I drown
But I never let it get me down
So when negativity surrounds
I know someday it will all turn around because
All my life I be waitin' for
I be prayin' for
For the people to say
That we don't want to fight no more
There be no more wars
And our children will play
One Day"

That day, that one day will come when we have achieved our
     goal
But don't start tomorrow to create change
to change yourself,
to change your view
Start today
Because tomorrow is not promised, for tonight maybe your last
Let's move on together
My brother and sister

Now back to the question I asked you in the beginning
Did you forget?
When we used to be one?

Alii, ngak a nglek a Chasmon Ongeu Tarimel. This is my second poem published and proud to express my knowledge of our Pacific people. I was born in Seattle, WA to Charles Ngiralengelang Tarimel and Monally Deureng Ridep. They migrated here in 1984 from the islands of Belau in the Western Pacific and continue to provide for my sisters, my niece, and myself. I am currently attending the University of Washington in Seattle majoring in American Ethnic Studies and English with a minor in Anthropology and Diversity. I hope to become an educator, working with youth to inspire and encourage young Pacific Islanders to achieve higher than what society says to be. A dios lomekngeltengat er kau ma kid el rokui el chad er a Vasa.

VASA II

Peni Tafuna

Visionaries

Ancestral

Sacred

Ambitious

Our people are Visionaries, we envisioned ourselves to stand tall in unity. For when we are united we become a force to be reckoned with. We always pay our respects to our Ancestral roots, for if it wasn't for them and their preservation of our cultural strength and wisdom we would not be the culturally empowered people we have come to be today. Our values is what we hold Sacred to us, because within those values lays the foundation that keeps our people afloat. Our people are Ambitious because we are forever striving to achieve what many try to keep from us. We are one people, with one voice, and if we stand together as one, we shall prevail.
This...is...Vasa...

The Importance of Vasa

Justin Dela Cruz

The ocean, it cradles the many islands. This concept shrouds the true identity of the islands being one. We are connected by the ocean, and we travel through this watery desert just as we do if we are on land. The importance of seeing the ocean as one big island is important because then we are not so separated from each other after all. Seeing the aspect of this conception brings many together, and we are able to unite our differences to become stronger as so called individuals. separation between islands by the sea causes us to become private, selfish, and secluded. As a result, it has created racism, class, discrimination, and many other ideas that forces us to pass judgement on people to separate ourselves. inversely, to imagine us all together in the pool that we call our ocean brings us closer than ever. For this reason, there is so many cultural influences within other cultures. In particular, the Filipino language, Tagalog, has traces of Middle-Eastern influence. We are then able to learn from and respect each other. I am able to see it within students at CCSF. I have noticed the importance of family and friends that has brought everyone so close together. I am a part of that, and I am able to learn from the many new friends. We are all here for each other. To our ancestors it was a way of life and a key part to survival. Thus, they were also able to create new relationships just like how we are at CCSF. By the way, it was my instructor who I appreciate dearly for giving me the opportunity to understand such a powerful notion: the vasa is our lens that helps us see beyond different waters, and we are connected by the vaka, our islands.

I am Filipino, and I was born here in the United States. My great-grandparents immigrated here because of the War in 1941 that had created the involvement of the Philippines. My great grandparents settlement here certainly changed the Filipino culture within the family. In my generation I cannot even speak my own language. However, I believe this does not separate myself from being a true Filipino because I am deeply interested to learn where I come from in the mainland, and to understand my people.

Our Sea of Islands

Ekekela Novero

The Maze in the Melting Pot

Ekekela Novero

Identity...
With multiple ethnicities
How do you identify in a society
where you're only allowed
the label of one race?
One face multiple sides:
my birth certificate claims American,
my blood says otherwise
Filipino, Samoan, Japanese, Tahitian, and German.

Those of identical descent may put in their two cents
and maybe in a sense...
you can relate to their story.
But when it comes to her story
does it ever really match with his story?
Ahh yes history..
they say it repeats but that each struggle is different
so to figure out who you are
do you become indifferent to one side of you?
How do you embrace the two
if one's traditions contradict the other
or your father's side has had more influence than your mother's..
Do you choose?

So many questions but no answers..
The problem: I thought my quest lay in

where I thought I should place myself in the ocean.
My mind was Americanized
and through American eyes
the vasa is what divides me.
No, the vasa is what unifies me.
One earth, one ocean.
One person, one identity.

Ekekela Novero was born and raised in San Francisco. She is of mixed descent, but mostly claims Filipino and Samoan. She is a biology major and pursuing a career in veterinarian medicine.

The Skin I'm In

Rovonne Allensworth

They misunderstand me because I fight for my race.
They look at me different cause the tone of my skin,
Or the way I dress the things I'm comfortable in.
They judge my family of different crime or different acts.
It should not matter if you're light, tan, or a hint of black.
I come from one race where they've been chain and tortured
And the other race where America views them for their
    agriculture.
I have visited my homelands and seen where my family was
    raised
I've seen what they have, and the kind of struggle they've faced.
I've tasted there food and how different it taste.
Also how joyful they are and the things they say.
I love to learn more about my history and myself.
Things that I can do for my culture and how I can help.

My family culture comes from the island of the Philippines and I am African
American and Filipino. The current place I live is in San Francisco of the
United States but my family is from the Philippines and they migrated over
here many years ago.

Identity Crisis

Leveti Tukumoeatu

How can one identify their self? The question can one be answered solely by the individual them self, not by others. When others attempt to identify another, it is purely a judgment they are making. The things they take into consideration when identifying a person is their clothing, their body language, the way they talk, who they associate their self with, etc. However, that is simply not enough.

What most people do not consider is the person's racial background or past. What someone goes through in the past definitely shapes who he or she are today. Someone who smiles every single day and goes happily through may have had a horrific past that is unknown. Someone who behaves in a violent way may be from the fact they were abused and or neglected as a child. In some way, a person's past reflects on the being they are today.

However, the main idea that everyone can reflect off of as to who they are retains to their culture. To pacific islanders, the ocean is everything. It gives reason for everything and life to everyone. It allows them to freely express themselves through words, music, and dance. It also allows them to be able to connect to the other fellow islands located nearby because they do not see the ocean as a barrier that separates them from each other, but a pathway that connects them.

My name is Leveti Tukumoeatu and I was born on July 5, 1993. My grandparents emigrated from the islands of Tonga and have lived in the United States long before I was born. I identify myself, as any individual should, just any ordinary human being who lives life day by day trying to make a happy living for myself.

Sometimes

Dwight Neal, Jr.

Sometimes your heart can lose its joy, and you wonder if you'll ever find it again.
Sometimes your spirit get's weak from the stress and strain of life and your load seems too heavy to bare....

But at times like this I want you to remember that the battle is not yours alone.
Hold on to your faith and remember what our ancestors/ocean went through, and believe in him the Lord, he is always willing and able to make everything alright.

My name is Dwight Neal Jr. and I am African American from San Francisco, CA. The U.S. is my native island where I have lived my whole life.

A Perfect Life

Ron Cruzado

To live and have a perfect life is something I do believe
I always think that it is possible and something that we can
achieve
I see a lot of people strive they do whatever it takes for their life
to be better
Somehow not everybody gets there
But still they never seem to surrender

I see myself as one of them
I try hard and I do my best
I work hard to tackle all the debacles no matter how tough it
gets
I don't give up easily and I don't let others pull me down
I always persevere for success even when my knees are about to
hit the ground

It's not easy to go through all the hardships that life throws at
you
But in order to be successful and great, you have to be ready to
face what is true
Truth being that nothing comes easy
If you want to succeed, you have to earn it
You have to do whatever it takes if you want to achieve
something that is worth it

Living and having a perfect life
It will always not be easy
You will have to face problems and difficulties before you can
taste it freely

But despite all the trouble, once you get there, it will be sweet
Because achieving something is way better if you know that you
have worked hard for it

I was born and raised in the island of the orient pearl, known as the
Philippine Islands. Though Filipino identity is still in question for many, I see
myself as an individual with Filipino roots that has a diverse understanding
of influence that has mold the Filipino culture. Now, the Golden state is
home, this land has given me more opportunity to understand further on how
VASA work its way on to people. This understanding is what I consider the
"ocean in me."

Taotao Manu Hao

Alyssa Indra Dutt Barcinas Seronio

You cannot determine who I am because of my skin color
I am Chamorro and Fijian
There is a part of me that connects me to our Vasa
My Chamorro culture has died down and I am unable to speak
my native tongue
I was raised speaking English
But that does not make me White
Regardless if I know my native tongue, my soul is forever
Chamorro and Fijian
Do not determine me as something I am not
Constantly teased because I look Indian instead of Chamorro
I am proud from who I came from
I am proud of my Chamorro Mother
She is always there to support and take care of her children
I am happy I came from My Fijian Father
Although I don't know too much about him
I carry my last name Barcinas-Seronio full of pride
Hoping that one day you will except me for who I am
Instead of what my skin color is

My name is Alyssa Indra Dutt Barcinas Seronio. I am Chamorro and Fijian.
My grandparents from my Chamorro side came from Guahan and my
grandparents on my Fijian side migrated from India to the Islands of Fiji.
Based on military stations my Chamorro and Fijian were stationed in
Monterey, CA, where they currently reside.

VASA

Thomas M. Patch

Our Journey unknown
Different and yet the same
The ocean shares us

My name is Thomas Patch, and I am Caucasian. I was born and raised in the United States and am currently working towards my BA in philosophy in San Francisco, California. I've always liked haiku as a poetry form because the format is so restrictive; it requires you to create a larger meaning outside the words.

Negro-pino

Damon Springfield

My nose was created to breathe the heat of my father's land.
I rise

My feet were designed to run the plains of my mother's land.
I thrive

Their hands worked hard just like their father's hands.
My drive

Their mothers provided the flavors of my flavor.
Good food

Respect them both through my behavior.
Never rude

Their parents came to this land they flew like wild vultures.
Through my blood I've heard the cries of two cultures.
Both tell me to get my education or go be a soldier.

I am black.
I am Filipino.
Two nationalities with personalities.

Biracial; I am African American and Filipino. I am both from Africa and the Philippines. My mother's family emigrated from Pangasinan, PI. I was born and raised in San Francisco, and relocated to Daly City several times. I now live in South San Francisco.

The Strength and Power of the Ocean

Gabriela Agosto

Gabriela Agosto was born in Puerto Rico in 1992. Currently an undergrad at CCSF, Mrs. Agosto plans to major in Graphic Design. Although not having any PI heritage, coming from an island and considering herself an islander allows her to relate to the love of the ocean.

World

Jessica David

How young can we be, in this world full of strangers?
Who would we be? Who really came first?
I'm just "that girl" speaking for young world,
Asking many questions with complicated words.
Simple questions indefinite answer,
God, yes indeed I'm a strong believer.
In this world were all brothers and sisters.
But why when u see her color u try to resist her?
There should be no discrimination in this world,
Our voices our notes, our writings shouldn't be insisted.
So just sit here and listen, maybe somehow you'll be delighted.
Tell me if u can't comprehend this world chain of fool
Most run around like there's no rules.
My heart, my mind my soul, my so called tools.
I might be young but I've been through a lot,
Situation sometimes too cold sometimes too hot.
With the mistakes and flaws,
There is choices, within our laws,
We can make better choices for our future.
It's not about the features,
It's about the internal. It's personality that measures
And life as we treasure.

I was born and raised in the Philippines. While growing up there I was taught the good manners and right conduct. I practice our cultures here in America. Growing up in 2 countries built me, made me who I am and shaped my view form of life.

Maps

Kee Hyun Lee

As accurate as they are,
As precise as they are,
As informative as they are,
They are not accurate,
They are not precise,
Nor are they informative.
You can see the entire world,
You can see continents,
You can see countries,
You can see states,
You can see islands.
But you cannot see culture,
You cannot see families,
You cannot see dance,
You cannot see joy,
You cannot see love.
Without a map, I felt a vibrant culture,
I felt Life.

My name is Kee Hyun Lee. I am currently a student at City College of San Francisco and I am also in Professor Palaita's Pacific Islanders Studies class. I have gained so much valuable information and insight being in his class.

My Ocean, Her Vasa

Marina Estrada

One beautiful evening, I was walking along the beach of San Francisco, letting the water splash against my thighs. I felt the soothing warmth of the sand beneath my toes. Oh how I love the beach. As I walked, I watched the sea glass glisten in the sunlight as it was setting, making them change color. When I looked up I saw a girl sitting in the sand cradling her knees between her arms crying. I first noticed how her hair was a massive ball of beauty and her skin was as dark and lovely as the sand. As I got closer to her she looked up at me, meeting my gaze. Her eyes were chocolate brown and filled with tears and loneliness. I sat next to her and asked, "Why are you crying? Are you lost? Do you need a ride home?" Hesitant, she looks down at the sand and whispers, "It's too far and I can't find it anymore."

Her words startled me. I couldn't imagine how I could help this girl or where I could find her family, so I said cautiously, "Well my house is by this beach. Just up the street around the corner. Do you live near the beach?" She stared up at me, tears streaming down her full cheeks. "I used to. I would play in the ocean every day. My Vasa was beautiful." She said wiping the tears from her face. "What is Vasa?" I ask curiously. "Vasa is my home", she smiled. "Vasa is my creator and my ocean", she smiled. Mystified by her response I sat silently listening to the rocking sounds of the ocean. I couldn't think of anything comforting to say.

She broke the silence and said, "My home is the island of Tahiti. It's in the Pacific Ocean just east from Tonga." I looked at her and smiled. "It must be beautiful." I said to her. "It is", she responded quietly. "You know, the good part about San Francisco, is that it's near the ocean. So, in a way, you have a part of your home here. I mean we do share the same ocean", I said proudly. "By the way, what is your name?" I asked. Looking astonished that I had asked, she said, "My name is Poema. In my culture it means Deep-Sea Pearl." She smiled. "Well my name is Marina and in my culture it means Of the Sea."

We both started giggling at how our names had so much in common even though we were born into different cultures. "See, our names are similar and we share the same ocean, the same home." I stated as I grabbed the water and let it fall between my fingers. The girl stared blankly at the ocean, as if looking for something in the distance. She turned to me, smiled and said, "It's not the same. This is my Vasa but it's not my land. This is not my home. It will never be my home."

My name is Marina Estrada. I am a Salvadorian/Mexican. I know nothing of my culture or how my family came to the United States. All I know is I was born and raised in San Francisco. My Father was born in El Salvador and my mom was born in Texas.

O le Vasa Vaesa'u

Filo Trevor Puni Vaesau

Vaesa'u... Not just a name
It's my life
My love
My sacred place
Vaesa'u is humble beginnings
Test filled roads
Bright futures
Vaesa'u is the seas traveled by my ancestors
The hope they brought with them
And the faith that willed them through
Vaesa'u not just a name.. It is my past, present, and future
It is the routes that have been mapped out by those before me
It is my keepsake
Vaesa'u... it is not only my name
It is my Love
My life
My Sacred Place.

My name is Filo Trevor Puni Vaesau, I am 20 years of age. I come from the island of American Samoa. Humbled by opportunities given to me in my life from those whose Faith keeps me alive. I know little of where I come from but know exactly where I am going.

From the Vasa to the Vasa

Kamiko Lozier

The continuous injection of western culture through militarization and social change is causing Pacific Island nations to lose their cultural identification. Additionally, the environmental impact of past nuclear testing is costing Pacific Islanders an irreplaceable and highly important resource, fertile land. Nonetheless, environmental, health and social problems have carved deep fissure into the Pacific Islanders cultures that are irreparable.

The Euro-American culture has been such a militarization force for the Pacific Islands that the shear influence has shifted the basic concepts of the Pacific Islands social structure. In the essay, S/Pacific N/oceans, by Professor Teresia Teaiwa PhD from the Victoria University, restates, "Clothing functioned as a devices of colonial social control, not only by eliminating nudity, but ... by distinguishing appropriate dress for [Pacific} islanders from appropriate dress from Europeans," (Teaiwa 97). As Professor Teaiwa emphasized that certain devices were used to control Pacific Islanders. The results of these devices can still be seen today as tourists are often associated with nudity and Pacific Islanders are modestly covered. The enforcement for these social controls was imposed on to the Pacific Islanders from the visual force that came from the bombardment of the Euro-American Army and Navy. As the military surveyed the island nations the idea that invasion would happen heighten the social transitions of the Pacific Islanders. Not only did social change affect the Pacific Islanders, but health issues also threaten the survival of the Pacific Islanders culture.

As nuclear testing in the Pacific Islands increased through the 20th century so did the overwhelming health problems from the harsh testing. One example, which has been examined over the years, is the American Nuclear testing in the Marshall Islands on Bikini Atoll. The American Government and Military used the Bikinians' devotion to God as a way for the U.S. to abdicate the Bikinians' homeland. As such Able and Castle Bravo, the nuclear bomb dropped on the Bikini Atoll, released radioactive material onto the island and into the ocean surrounding the island. Furthermore, from the radioactive material, "Numerous claims had been filed against the United States as the [Bikinians] became afflicted with radioactivity-related cancers and birth defects," (91 Teaiwa) leading to the trust to the Bikinians from the United States. However, even with more money to researcher the effect of the nuclear testing, large numbers of Pacific Islanders die without any knowledge of how the radioactive material might have affected them. This devastation is slowly pushing the survival of the native Pacific Islanders culture to its limits.

Nonetheless, the biggest threat to the Pacific Islanders culture is environmental problems. As each island in the Pacific has limited space, the cultural concepts the Pacific Islanders beliefs allow everyone the right to everything around them including the Vasa (oceans). For example, Hawai'i natives believe that the Hawai'i Islands belong to the community and should be shared with everyone. But as Missionaries began to pressure the Big Island's Chief, the land became privatized in 1848, (Act of War: the Overthrow of the Hawai'i Nation 1993). In addition, Hawaiian natives no longer control their own homeland. But the Missionaries enforced the idea of privatized land through military present on the coast of the Hawai'i Islands. Now the Big Island, Hawai'i is overwhelmingly populated by foreign visitors, who take the land and destroy it slowly. The Hawaiian ecosystem has been stretched to the extreme to support a population of non-natives that don't reinvest into the environment. As such the native Hawaiians value of land, ocean, and sky around Hawai'i is lost pushing Pacific cultures towards extinction.

In conclusion, many factors affect the survival of the Pacific Islander cultures and allow for the Pacific Island nations to lose their cultural grounds. However, the biggest loss of cultural identity comes from the militarization still occurring in combination with the nuclear testing that occurred on the Islands. These issues of militarization and past nuclear testing which lead to environmental, health and social problems will continue to push Pacific Island cultures to the point of disrepair.

Rise Up and Remember

Amelia Vunipola

My brothers and sisters RISE UP
Embrace what was handed to you
Respect what is in you
Love what is running through you
You are the ocean and the ocean is you

Remember who you are
Remember what was taught to you
Remember what's embedded in you
Remember what's surrounding you
You are the ocean and the ocean is you

Rise up to the challenge
Rise up and claim your culture
For it will always be a part of you
What you say and what you do
You are the ocean and the ocean is you

You're in America, it's not in you
To be yourself you must look back
To your birth, even before that
Our history is lies within us
You are the ocean and the ocean is you

RISE UP AND REMEMBER

My name's Amelia Vunipola and I attend City College of San Francisco. I was born and raised in the Bay Area but the Kingdom of Tonga is and will forever by home. As the Coat of arms state, "Koe 'Otua mo Tonga ko hoku tofi'a."

Through Our Own Eyes

Tiffany Mariano

We see who we are in our own eyes.
But we are constantly being told many lies.

You know who are, I am Filipino, Russian
There really is no discussion

But why are we letting other define us
Letting them make a huge fuss

Be proud for who you are,
Only you will never stray afar.

Be true to yourself, only you know
You are the highest, nothing close to low

Don't like no one tell you else wise
Only your heart knows the true size

You are who you are, nothing can change that

My name is Tiffany Mariano, I am Filipino, Russian. I grew up in Daly City, California and been here my whole life. Although born American, I still practice my Filipino culture and identify with it.

Through Experience, I Will Know

Ramses Mariscal

From experience, I will know how it feels,
How it feels to travel upon hundreds of miles,
Knowing in any moment, it can all end.
I will know the greatest moment of it all, the moment when it's
    over.
Books and imagination paint a vague glimpse of the journey
    thousands of people take.
A journey that those touched only get to see light.
To the land of abundance and novelty.
Being from their destination, I can never fully grasp their
    struggle
I am from this land, so called rich.
But they say, I am not one of them.
They see me through the eyes of a beggar, and I'm the prince,
    breastfed on all occasions.
I don't disagree.
But I too have worked; maybe not to the same degree.
There's no need for me to move.
Many say I'm lucky.
I agree and am fully grateful.
I've been tasked to learn where I'm from and to become one of
    them.
Tasked not from insistence, but for my own self awareness.
Books teach you history, images give you vision.
But experience is the journey.
Only through experience, will I know where my people are
    from and the struggles they go through.

I was born and raised in San Francisco, California. My parents are immigrants from Mexico. It's not enough for me to say I'm Mexican American when I'm fully embedded in American culture, but I am grateful for knowing to speak my parent's native language and sharing their cultural traditions.

Invisible Divisible

Monica Reyes

There are people of different shaded faces,
But still they are people of the same races.
Separated physically by the white colored wall,
Sitting "together" as one in the same hall.
Three tiny groups became two,
I always ask which one do I belong to?
It sucks to be in the middle where I am caught,
Both groups love each other, so I thought.
I'm in the middle of the ride,
Everything's going to be alright.
That's how time goes,
Evolution grows.
Why do we only talk when you are in need?
It all hurts the same as we are left to bleed.
For the rest of the world to change,
We need to start and rearrange.
If we can't get along, then there's no hope for the rest,
Getting along with no division will be our greatest test.
I'm not saying we physically fight or hate,
We just need to get rid of this invisible gate,
That stands just between us two,
So we can be whole like the ones I knew.

My name is Monica Reyes and I was born and raised in California. Both my parents are from the province of Bataan, Philippines. I currently reside in Daly City, CA.

VASA

Hannelore Rehbock

VASA, an ocean so vast and so bottomless.
VASA, an ocean that contains many stories.
VASA, an ocean where my ancestors rest.
VASA, the pathway to each island.
VASA, my life line.
VASA, an ocean that is within me,
Flows through my body and gives me a feeling of renewal
VASA, I am one with you.

My name is Hannelore Rehbock, and I identify as Samoan, Hawaiian, and Japanese. I was adopted by a Japanese mother and German-Argentine father. I have lived in San Francisco my whole life.

Never Ended, Always Regret

Aung K. Lin

Just more than to be called as Islands,
Colonialist saw them as if there seemed none of them…
Having no oceanic lens is somehow, a disturbance,
Well, you would not believe Islander's mutual existence…

People being forced to contact with colonial discourses,
Don't know how, islanders would accept your way of
preaches…
Please, let them follow their pursuit of happiness,
Even though, you've declared people's rights in Amendments,
Just to clarify that, Islanders boiled in hatred,
It's a shame for you to slaughter like craziness…
This is not your burden of carving Islanders art of
omnipotence…
They already had adopted their unique way of practices,
Not just like privatizing land for the sake of business,
To let you know that, withdraw your thousands of madness…

A miserable relentless for me to continue my poem,
It's a nightmare to not share Islander's mayhem...
How awesome, Islander can navigate without a map,
Cannot imagine, when Colonialist lost a map, on their way
back…

It's time for you to payback the lives of Bikinians,
OMG, the story had been distorted by intense sexism.
The source is linked by the voyage of Christopher Columbus,
An honor, for the bravery to face the gun with mightiness,
This is the truth of the Islander's with pristine sadness,

Please do not forget how you got independence,
Ancestor sacrificed for the continuation of our existence....

My name's Aung K. Lin, and I am an International student. I'm currently pursuing higher education focusing on business management. I've excavated remorse feeling of how Islander's resist the tremendous action against the colonialist, which drew my attention of getting to know the precise definition of how large the VASA network exists.

Identity with Oceania

Vincent R. Arroyo

Identity is like a puzzle, every piece has its place. If someone tries to force a piece into a place where it does not belong or tries to make that puzzle look different, it damages the puzzle and all of its pieces. To the point where that whole picture is blurred. Having an identity, a place in the world, is very important to everyone. Weather its gay or straight, New Yorker or San Franciscan, Hawai'ian or Sāmoan, everyone just wants to fit into their own place or group. If that group is "damaged" it is hard for the people to identify themselves with in that group.

This is similar to what has happened in history to the Native Americans, African Tribes, and especially Pacific Islanders. These groups were thought of as below standards and forces to change their way of life to even be close to what "more advance" groups thought were acceptable. Within these changes, they lost their sense of identity. There for, having an Oceanic view, in a way, changes how we view ourselves and the world. Having this view empowers you, it makes you stand up and be proud, even when you're being put down for your differences.

In Epeli Hau'ofa's paper *"Our Sea of Islands"* it proves that very point. Professor Hau'ofa starts out by saying that he had succumb to the belittlement and judgment of the pacific. That they are "...much too small, too poorly endowed with resources, and too isolated from the centers of economic growth for their inhabitant ever to be able to rise above their preset condition of dependence on the largesse of wealthy nations" (4). He tried to find the bright side to this ugly pictorial that had been mocked up by European discovers and American leaders.

It took having to see students of his being belittled by what he was teaching them, to change his view.

He says that even though most of Oceania lives in "tiny confined space" they think of themselves as "a sea of islands" and not "islands in a far seas," which is empowering to them. By the end of the paper he changes his tone on smallness completely, states that "We must not allow anyone to belittle us again, and take away our freedom."(page16). Freedom being of our identities and seeing ourselves as people of the world.

One thing that was brought up through discussions on this topic in my *Pacific Islanders Class*, was the theme of "Smallness is a state of mind" (which also came up in Malcolm X's speech *"Not just an American problem, but a world problem"*). This idea can be very poisonous to the people who live in "smaller" countries/islands. This way of thinking can come from a number of sources, but the most harmful is from ourselves. If you think small you are small, but people with in that situation can change their thinking, but they have to do something about it. While in this discussion, Professor Palaita said " You can't talk shit, about shit, and not do shit." If you do not change your way of thinking of the world, and try to do something to make a difference, then you cannot complain about it.

Coming from a mixed background, I have struggled with this issue of judgment and belittlement that Hauʻofa discussed in his essay. Society thinks that I am out of place among my family, friends, and other social groups. Society wants to just make me one thing, they say I am white because of my skin tone, or I am Mexican because of my last name. Even to this day there's no clear place for me in others eyes, but I know where I belong. I do identify myself as Hawaiʻian, Portuguese, French, and Mexican, it doesn't matter if I can speak the language or if I eat the food, all that matters is that I can identify myself within that group/s. Having an Oceanic view (or what could even be called a World View) I can be proud of my mix heritage. That's what everyone wants to feel, they want to feel like they are a part of something bigger then themselves. They want to be a part of the puzzle, what we know as the world.

I was born and raised in San Francisco. My Father and his family is Mexican-immigrants. My Mother's Mother is of Hawai'ian and Portuguese ancestry from the big island of Hawai'i and my Mother's Father is from France.

No One To Blame

Matthew David Palaita

I was born on January 22, 1982
The crime & time is what I've been through

In my family I was the black sheep
Forever drinking & smoking trying to be discreet

In my past gangs & alcohol is what I knew
Always out late passed my curfew

I have always been in trouble being an outlaw
Gangs & alcohol had been my downfall

I had hit rock bottom at the age of seventeen
I got into a fight that led to a crime scene

Throughout my troubles there were none of my friends
My family had forever been there to the end

Mom had always said, "Friends every day, but family is
forever."
My parents was always there to keep the family together

Through my tragedy mom was always down & sad
I sometimes wished I took the advice from mom & dad

For my actions I have caused nothing but pain
For what I've done I will never be the same

Throughout my devastation
God & my family had always been my inspiration

I've been gone away from my family for so many years
Mom, I apologize for causing you so many tears

I give thanks to God for blessing me through my trials &
tribulation
I give thanks to my family for loving me through my
humiliation

I also give thanks to Gabby, my beautiful wife,
For always putting up with my crazy life

Throughout the pain & suffering there was no laughter
I have learned from my past to live a new chapter

Thank you Jehovah for helping me change
Throughout my adversity there is no one to blame!

I am Matthew David Palaita. After spending more than a decade in prison, I realized how much I've been missing. The ocean has really become a deep sense of inspiration for me and it is there I am heading.

A Love for Ocean

Alexia Diaz

Waves crash and the collision is chaotic
The sounds of fury and calm is all a state of mind
Knowledge and Truth are the essential supplements to one's
body,   mind and soul.
I am Ocean. Love. Passion.Vasa. Product of my ancestresses.
Self fulfillment, Self reflection, reclaiming the tongues ripped
away   from strangers of distant lands. Melodies, Patterns,
Food,   Stories, Prayers, Dances.
All reminders of our struggles and monumental achievements to
          resistances.
When the storms and tides are wild and free ripping what men
have   made.
Humility, Respect, Unification is once again called on by Vasa
to   us.
Remind. Educate. Pass on the knowledge for the generations to
          come.
Please don't forget your ancestors.
Please don't forget your histories.
Please don't forget your culture.
Please don't forget you.
I am.
You are.
We are.
Vasa.

Alexia Diaz is an honored student of City College of San Francisco's
Interdisciplinary Studies, Pacific Islanders in the U.S. class. A native to San
Francisco, CA., Alexia is a Filipino Nicaraguan American, who thrives in the
search for what it means to be a multiracial, young, educated woman. With
this piece she hopes to always remind individuals, and other individuals like
her, we are always forever changing, forever evolving, and VASA is us.

Epilogue: Ua Gaepu le Vai

Andrew Fatilua Tunai Tuala

An historic event of epic proportions took place at Treasure Island in San Francisco, CA. On August 2nd of this year, a fleet of Pacific Voyagers representing several Pacific island nations—Fiji, Samoa, Tonga, Aotearoa, Tahiti, Hawai'i, Micronesia—voyaged the Pacific carrying a central yet unifying message about the place most Pacific Islanders call home—the ocean.

In light of this message, Pacific Islanders from across the San Francisco Bay area congregated on Treasure Island to welcome and acknowledge our seafaring families after months out at sea. Members of our communities—children, elders, supporters, allies—came to witness an aspect of our culture that in recent years has begun to erode from the memories of our ancestors. The arrival of these canoes or waka (wha-kah) is a testament to the hope and the determination of keeping a centuries-old knowledge of celestial navigation alive, despite its struggle.

As the fleet approached a secluded beach on the eastern side of Treasure Island, cries of happiness can be heard surrounding the area while tears of joy fill the eyes of our elders. And as the crews disembarked from their wakas, greetings from every Pacific Island language can be heard, while gifts of dance, song, and prayer were shared. Special dignitaries from the Samoan community like Rev. Moegagogo Tamasese, Manufou Liaiga Anoa'i, and Ace Tago, to name a few, served on various committees to welcome the Gaualofa crew of Samoa and the rest of the Pacific Voyagers.

As Pacific Islander students at the City College of San Francisco, the privilege to take part in this event was a learning experience. Numerous Pacific Island organizations came together for this event despite the challenges of organizing so many different groups. Even as conflicts arose, members our communities maintained our dignity and our humility as values from the ocean we come from. The chance to be a part of this great work becomes real for many of us and it is particularly why our families of Pacific Voyagers acknowledge the immensity of our spatial relationships. We witnessed that our ocean/vasa "is a space that relates rather than separates."

The Pacific Voyagers brought to San Francisco and the greater Bay Area a sense of pride, as well as a sense of urgency to the state of our Samoan community, particularly our youth. Social and cultural challenges are becoming even more difficult to address such as the low retention from schools and colleges to high incarceration rates. But despite that, the voyager's visit to our great city reaffirmed one thing: the significance of the power of will and love in meeting the needs of our growing communities. Perhaps this has been their compass throughout this journey; it has been the central guide to a successful arrival; it has been the currents and the waves that have kept them moving; It is exactly what we need if we are to navigate difficult terrain in the coming years.

We've always wondered what great power would propel our people to encounter the largest living entity in the world— our ocean? The answer can be found in a simple yet meaningful statement by a Samoan chief of Samoa's Independence movement of the 1930's: "We are moved by love, but never by intimidation.

Knowledge

Va'eomatoka "Toka" Valu

When we think of the term "diaspora" as it pertains to a specific population or group of people, we often tend to attach physical distance and space as key parts of the discussion that is generated from it. However, "time" is a concept that has been a part of Pacific Islander knowledge for many generations before European settlers arrived on our shores and is also a tangible and substantial variable that should be included in all discourses surrounding the diaspora of Pacific peoples.

The cover illustration is my analysis of that discourse. The boy on the left represents vibrancy and the energy that is inherent in all youth. The designs surrounding him aren't bounded or restrained and are boldly colored which echoes the passion that embodies many of our Pacific Islander brothers and sisters today currently living in the "diaspora." Together, they represent a generation of scholars, artists, performers and pioneers who are not afraid to make sure that their voices and their concerns are heard and properly addressed.

The old man to the right, is drawn on tapa (look closely, you'll see it's Tongan ngatu) which is a common commodity and symbol of long held knowledge in many cultures across Oceania. The old man is the boy now aged, withered and tired from a life full of struggle and resistance. Notice that I never mention that the boy, now a "tangata 'eiki" (old man in Tongan) had ever reached the goal he had fought for all through the years. The point here is that our struggle as Pacific Islanders, fighting for visibility in a world that largely disregards or devalues our existence, is an on-going and perpetual one. One that needs inspired and motivated pioneers to carry on when our generation fades into memory. Last but not least, the designs surrounding the old man are rigid, fading and softly colored in comparison to those surrounding the boy. The solid blacks, sharp edges and warm colors indicate a lifelong collection of knowledge that is now firmly a part of his being and hopefully disseminated amongst a new generation of inspired leaders.

Holistically, the piece speaks to how our people, armed with Pacific knowledge that has traveled great lengths, have adapted themselves in order to succeed not only across the physically and sometimes finite spans of distance, but also across the endless expanse of space, time, and generations.

The 4th Annual Pacific Islander
Talanoa Series:
Honoring Our Culture, Honoring Our Women
Fall 2011

Manufou Liaiga Anoa'i
"Pacific Islander Women & Politics"

Kerri Ann Borja-Navarro
"Militarization in Guahan & Oceania"

Joanne Rondilla
"Skin-Lightening in the Philippines"

Natalie Bartley-Ah Soon & Taunu'u Ve'e
"Issues in Pacific Islander Community Health"

Fealofani Bruun & Lauaki Jackie Selinger
"Reviving Celestial Navigation across Oceania"

Kapi'olani Lee
"Pacific Islanders in the Media"

Malissa Netane
"Domestic Violence in Pacific Communities"

The Pacific Islander community thanks the above individuals
for sharing their expertise and stories at our 2011 Fall Talanoa
Series at the City College of San Francisco.

Your contribution to our field of knowledge continues to inspire,
motivate, and teach our children for oceans and generations to
come.

About the Editors

Kerri Ann Borja Navarro is a member of the Chamoru organization Famoksaiyan. She recently received a Master's Degree in Education from San Francisco State University with a focus on indigenous Pacific Islander Education.

Richard Benigno Cantora is currently the Coordinator of the Students Supporting Students (S-CUBE) and co-founder of the Filipino-American Student Success Center Tulay (Bridge) program at the City College of San Francisco. Rick plans to pursue a doctoral degree in Ethnic Studies.

Andrew Fatilua Tunai Tuala is currently pursuing an Associate's Degree in Public Administration from the City College of San Francisco. He has recently relocated home to Apia, Samoa.

Vaeomatoka "Toka" Valu is currently a Pacific Islander outreach recruiter in the office of admissions at the University of Washington, Seattle. He received a Bachelor's Degree in Art from the University of Washington.

David Ga'oupu Palaita (vika) is currently an adjunct professor of Interdisciplinary Studies and Pacific Islander Studies at the City College of San Francisco. He is currently spearheading the movement to create the college's associate degree program in Pacific Islands Studies.

Made in the USA
Middletown, DE
27 September 2021